Colophon

© 2003 Rebo International b.v., Lisse, The Netherlands

This 2nd edition reprinted in 2006.

Original recipes and photos: © R&R Publishing Pty. Ltd.

Design, layout and typesetting: R&R Publishing Pty. Ltd., Victoria, Australia

Cover design: Minkowsky Graphics, Enkhuizen, The Netherlands

ISBN 13: 978-90-366-1605-8

ISBN 10: 90-366-1605-0

now you're cookin'
STARTERS

THIS BOOK JUST MAKES YOU WANNA COOK -

REBO
PUBLISHERS

Preface

Shrimp cocktail: for years this was the most popular and often only starter on the menu. Fortunately, times have changed, and our cuisine has taken on an international flavor. That is where this cookbook full of inspirational starters from the kitchens of the world comes in: *Bulgur Wheat Salad with Grilled Peppers*, *Mediterranean Spinach and Herb Roulade*, *Chicken Yakitori*. Perhaps you would like breadsticks wrapped in Parmesan ham, or crispy vegetables with a Provençal anchovy dip or some delicious hummus? What will it be? Shall we proceed to the main course, or shall we sneak in another starter?

Abbreviations

All measurements conform to European
and American measurement systems.
For easier cooking, the American cup
measurement is used throughout the book.

tbsp = tablespoon

tsp = teaspoon

oz = ounce

lb = pound

°F = degrees Fahrenheit

°C = degrees Celsius

g = gram

kg = kilogram

cm = centimeter

ml = mililiter

l = liter

Method

Place the bulgur wheat in a bowl and pour over boiling water to about 1in/2cm above the level of the bulgur wheat and leave to soak for 20 minutes. Meanwhile, preheat the grill to high. Grill the yellow peppers, skin-side up, for 15-20 minutes, until the skin has blistered and blackened all over. Transfer to a plastic bag, seal, and leave to cool. When cold enough to handle, remove, and discard the charred skins and roughly chop the flesh.

Blanch the green beans in boiling water for 3-4 minutes, drain, refresh under cold running water and set aside. Put the tomatoes into a bowl, cover with boiling water and leave for 30 seconds. Peel, deseed, then roughly chop the flesh.

Combine the ingredients for the dressing and mix well. Drain the bulgur wheat and transfer to a salad bowl. Add the dressing and toss well. Add the vegetables, scallions, brazil nuts, parsley, and seasoning and gently toss together to mix.

Ingredients

8oz/225g bulgur wheat

2 yellow peppers, quartered
and deseeded

9oz/250g pack green beans, halved

2 ripe tomatoes

4 callions, sliced

3oz/75g brazil nuts, roughly chopped

4 tbsp chopped fresh parsley

sea salt and freshly ground

black pepper

For the dressing

4 tbsp extra virgin olive oil

1 tbsp wholegrain mustard

1 clove garlic, crushed

1 tsp balsamic vinegar

1 tsp white wine vinegar

Bulgur Wheat Salad with Grilled Peppers

Method

Assemble all the ingredients in a large salad bowl in the order they are listed. Dress the salad with the vinaigrette at the table just before serving.

Salade Niçoise

Ingredients

lettuce leaves, washed and dried

6½oz/185g can tuna

3 potatoes, cooked and quartered

2 hard-boiled eggs, quartered

3 tomatoes, quartered

12 black olives, cored

9oz/250g green beans, blanched

6 anchovy fillets, drained

½ cucumber, sliced

For the dressing

2 tbsp wine vinegar

1 tsp Dijon mustard

salt and pepper

6 tbsp olive oil

1 tsp tarragon, finely chopped

1 tsp chervil, finely chopped

starters

Method

To make the dressing: place the lemon juice, garlic, tahini paste

and 3 tablespoons of water in a food processor and blend until smooth.

Alternatively, combine with a fork. Season to taste.

Toss together the carrots, celery heart, and apples and transfer

to individual serving bowls. Drizzle over the dressing.

Ingredients

3 carrots, grated

1 celery heart, thinly sliced

2 eating apples, peeled, cored,

and thinly sliced

For the dressing

3 tbsp lemon juice

1 clove garlic, crushed

2 tbsp tahini paste

salt

Celery, Carrot, and Apple Salad with Tahini

Method

Beat eggs well then add scallions, flour, bacon, stock,

and salt and combine to form a smooth batter.

Add 2 teaspoons of oil to a 10in/25cm frying pan on medium

heat and spread over base of pan. Pour a quarter of the batter

into the pan, also ensuring it covers the base.

When pancake edge is golden, turn pancake carefully until cooked.

Remove and repeat the procedure 3 more times with extra oil

to yield 4 pancakes.

Serve hot cut into slices.

Ingredients

2 eggs

6 scallions, sliced finely

1⅓ cup flour

2 slices bacon, finely chopped

1 cup chicken stock

pinch of salt

3 tbsp vegetable oil

Peking Scallion Pancakes

Method

To curing beef: place sugar, salt, peppercorns, and thyme leaves on a large plate. Roll beef in mixture several times to coat and form a crust. Place beef on a rack set in a shallow dish. Cover. Refrigerate for 24 hours–check from time to time that the crust is still encasing the meat as the juices that are released during marinating may loosen it.

Wipe away all of the herb crust thoroughly when ready using absorbent paper towel. Using a very sharp knife, cut beef across the grain into paper-thin slices–this is easier to do if you place the fillet in the freezer for 10 minutes before slicing. Place slices on a plate. Cover. Refrigerate until ready to use.

To make the scones: preheat oven to 400°F/210°C. Lightly spray or brush a baking tray with unsaturated oil. Set aside.

Sift flour and baking powder together into a large bowl. Add olives, basil, and black pepper to taste. Mix to combine. Make a well in the center. Place milk and mustard in a small bowl; whisk to combine. Pour into well in flour mixture. Mix quickly to make a soft dough. Turn dough onto a lightly floured surface. Knead briefly until smooth.

Press mixture or roll out to form a 1in/2cm thick rectangle. Using a 1½ in/3cm scone cutter, cut out scones. Place on prepared baking tray with sides just touching. Bake for 10-12 minutes or until scones are well–risen and golden. Transfer to a wire rack. Cool slightly.

To serve, cut scones and spread with a little chutney. Top with a small mound of beef and a thyme sprig.

Ingredients

chutney of your choice	3 tbsp crushed black peppercorns
fresh thyme sprigs	1 large bunch fresh thyme,
thyme cured beef	leaves only
¾ cup sugar	7oz/200 g lean beef fillet,
½ cup salt	trimmed of visible fat

Olive Scones with Thyme Cured Beef

Olive Scones

2 cups plain flour

2 tsp baking powder

¼ cup black olives, rinsed

drained, and chopped

1 tbsp chopped fresh basil

freshly ground black pepper

1 cup buttermilk

1 tbsp Dijon mustard

starters

15

Makes **24 small skewers**

Method

Soak 24 small or 8 large bamboo skewers in cold water for at least 20 minutes. Preheat a barbecue or grill to a high heat.

Cut each calamari ring in half. Thread strips onto bamboo skewers in an "S" shape—use 1 strip on small skewers and 3 strips on large skewers.

Place skewers on barbecue or under grill. Cook, turning several times, for 1-2 minutes or until calamari is just cooked.

To make the teriyaki sauce: place shallot, ginger, vinegar, soy sauce, honey and 1 tablespoon lime juice in a small saucepan over medium heat.

Stir in sesame oil and remaining lime juice. Serve with skewers. If serving as a light meal, accompany with a tossed green salad. The skewers are delicious warm or cold.

Ingredients

2 large calamari (squid) tubes, cleaned, cut into thin rings

Teriyaki Sauce

1 shallot, thinly sliced

1 tsp minced fresh ginger

¼ cup rice wine vinegar or sherry

2 tbsp reduced–salt soy sauce

1 tsp honey

2 tbsp lime or lemon juice

1 tsp sesame oil

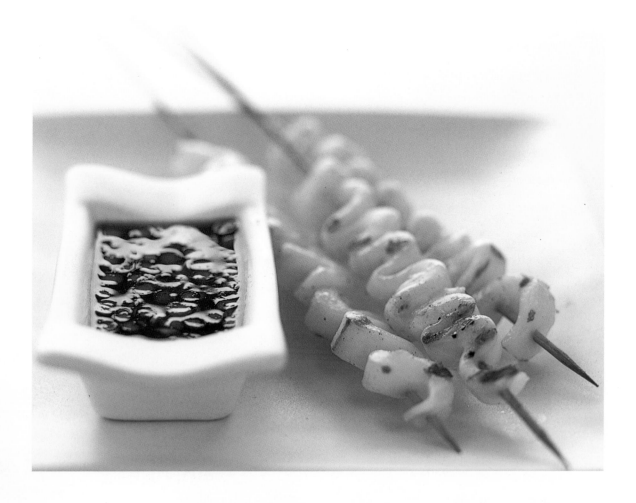

Teriyaki Calamari Skewers

Method

Preheat the oven to 375°F/180°C.

Bring a large pot of salted water to a boil and add the pasta shells (boiling until they are just tender). Drain and allow the pasta shells to cool.

Squeeze the defrosted spinach dry and transfer to a large bowl. Quickly blanch the baby spinach leaves in hot water, then drain and add to the frozen spinach. Add the finely chopped Spanish onion, ricotta, grated Parmesan, fennel, basil and garlic, then mix thoroughly. Add salt and pepper (to taste).

Heat the olive oil in a deep saucepan and add the chopped scallions. Sauté for 2 minutes (until softened), then add the chopped tomatoes, sugar, and salt and pepper (to taste) and simmer for 30 minutes (until the tomatoes have liquified). Add the dill, stirring thoroughly, then season (to taste) with additional salt and pepper if necessary. Set aside.

Spoon the spinach mixture into the pasta shells, adding just enough to fill each shell. Set aside.

Divide the tomato sauce among six ovenproof dishes and place five filled pasta-shells on top of the sauce in each dish. Sprinkle with extra Parmesan cheese, cover the dishes with foil, and bake at 375°F/180°C for 20 minutes. Remove the foil and bake for an additional 5 minutes (or until golden).

Ingredients

30 jumbo pasta shells

1lb/500g frozen chopped spinach, thawed

1 large handful of fresh baby spinach leaves

1 small Spanish onion, finely chopped

1lb/500g ricotta cheese, fresh

4oz/120g grated Parmesan, fresh

2 tbsp fennel seeds

20 fresh basil leaves, chopped

3 cloves garlic, minced

1 tbsp olive oil

6 scallions (chopped)

3lb/1.5kg tomatoes (fresh)

1 tbsp sugar

salt and lots of freshly ground black pepper

2 tbsp fresh dill, chopped

additional Parmesan cheese (to serve)

Spinach-Stuffed Pasta Shells with Tomato Sauce

starters

Method

Toast the bread, then brush with a little oil. Meanwhile, beat together the ricotta and pesto, then stir in the rest of the oil. Season with pepper.

Cut the toast into fingers, discarding the ends. Spread over the ricotta mixture and shave over the Parmesan, using a vegetable peeler.

Toast Fingers with Pesto and Ricotta

Ingredients

12 slices speciality bread,

such as Grande Rustique, sliced

3 tbsp olive oil

½ lb/250g tub ricotta

5 tbsp pesto

black pepper

2 tbsp Parmesan

Method

Cut off the artichoke stalks, so that the artichokes stand flat. Place in a large saucepan of boiling salted water and simmer, partly covered, for 40 minutes or until tender. To test if the artichokes are cooked, pull off an outside leaf – it should pull away easily.

Remove the artichokes from the pan and set aside for 30 minutes to cool. Meanwhile, make the sauce. Mix together the sour cream, scallions, vinegar, and garlic. Pull the central cone of leaves out of each artichoke, leaving a wall of leaves around the edge, and discard.

Scrape away the inedible core with a teaspoon, to leave the edible base.

Spoon plenty of sauce into the artichoke center. Place the artichokes on plates and eat by plucking out a leaf and dipping it into the sauce.

Use your teeth to pull away the edible fleshy part at the base of the leaf, then discard the rest.

Artichokes with Sour Cream Sauce

Ingredients

4 large globe artichokes

1⅓ carton soured cream

5 scallions, finely chopped

1 tbsp balsamic vinegar

1 clove garlic, finely chopped

salt

Method

To make the blinis: place yeast, sugar and ½ cup of the milk in a small bowl. Stand for 5 minutes or until frothy.

Place buckwheat and plain flours in a large bowl. Mix to combine. Make a well in the center. Pour yeast mixture and remaining milk into well. Mix until just combined.

Place egg white in a separate clean bowl. Beat until soft peaks form.

Fold egg mixture into batter. Season with black pepper to taste.

Heat a nonstick frying pan over a medium heat. Lightly spray or brush with unsaturated oil. Place tablespoons of mixture in pan—you should be able to cook 5-6 blinis at a time in a 20-23cm frying pan. Cook for 1-2 minutes or until bubbles appear on the surface. Turn over. Cook second side for 30 seconds or until golden.

Place on absorbent paper towel. Keep warm in a low oven while cooking the remaining mixture.

Serve blinis warm or cold topped with a spoonful of yogurt cheese and a low–fat topping of your choice, if desired—shown here topped with semi-dried tomatoes.

Blinis with Herbed Yogurt Cheese

Ingredients

½ quantity yogurt cheese flavored with

1 tbsp chopped fresh dill

and 1 tbsp chopped

fresh mint

Blinis

1 tsp dry yeast

1 tsp sugar

1½ cups low fat milk, warmed

1 cup buckwheat flour

½ cup plain flour

1 egg white

freshly ground black pepper

Yogurt Cheese

1lb/6oz low fat yogurt

chopped fresh seasoning

ground spices

shredded Spanish pepper

grated vegetables

Construction

Line a colander with a double thickness of cheesecloth or muslin. Place over a large bowl. Spoon in yogurt. Cover with plastic food wrap. Stand in the refrigerator overnight.

Transfer yogurt to a clean bowl. Discard whey. Add seasonings of your choice to cheese. Mix to combine. Store cheese in an airtight container in the refrigerator for up to 1 week.

Makes 1 cup

starters

Method

Slice each eggplant vertically into six thin slices. Salt lightly and allow the bitter juices to drain for 30 minutes. Rinse briefly and drain well.

Slice two large sides off each pepper (and reserve the remainder for another use).

Place the pepper slices under a hot grill and cook until the skins are blackened. Place the black peppers into a double-thickness plastic bag and seal, allowing them to steam. Set aside for thirty minutes. When cool enough to handle, open the bag and gently peel-off and discard the black pepper skins. Allow the pepper flesh to cool.

Heat a grill and lightly brush or spray the eggplant with oil. Grill the eggplant pieces until golden, then turn and brush with olive oil. Grill second side until golden (about 3 minutes each side). Allow to cool.

Meanwhile, in a bowl or food processor, combine the feta cheese, ricotta cheese and herbs, with salt and pepper (to taste). (If using a processor, take care not to over-process – the cheese mixture should not be "sloppy").

To assemble, lie each eggplant slice on your work-surface and top with a large piece of pepper. Place a generous spoonful of the cheese filling on top of the pepper (near the bottom end closest to you) and add 4 rocket or spinach leaves over the cheese. From the cheese-end, roll up firmly but gently, making sure that some of the rocket or spinach protrudes from each end. Serve drizzled with parsley pesto.

To make the parsley pesto: pack everything (except the oil) into a food processor and process. With the motor running, add just enough oil to combine the pesto.

Ingredients

For Rolls

2 large smooth eggplants

6 large peppers, red or yellow

1-2 tbsp olive oil

5oz/150g feta cheese

7oz/200g ricotta cheese

20 basil leaves

10 mint leaves

1 bunch of rocket

(or handful of baby spinach)

salt and pepper (to taste)

Stuffed Eggplant Rolls with Parsley Pesto

For Pesto

2 cups Italian parsley

2 cloves garlic

1 tbsp red wine vinegar

1 tsp anchovy paste

⅓ cup olive oil

Method

To make the batter: lightly whisk together the eggs and water, then pour onto the flour all at once and whisk quickly, until the batter is smooth.

Heat the cranberry and orange sauce in a small saucepan, over a gentle heat, until warm and runny. Remove from the heat and place in a bowl.

Heat 2in/5cm of oil in a wok or frying pan. Dip the vegetables into the batter and coat well. Test the temperature of the oil by dropping in a little batter, if it floats straight back to the surface the oil is hot enough.

Deep-fry the vegetables in small batches for 3-4 minutes or until crisp and golden. Remove with a slotted spoon and drain on paper towel. Season with salt. If using, deep-fry a few basil leaves for 20 seconds, until crisp. Serve the vegetables at once with the dipping sauce.

Ingredients

2 eggs

½ cup ice-cold water

½ cup plain white flour, sieved

8oz/225g jar cranberry and orange sauce, for dipping

vegetable oil, for deep-frying

1 eggplant, cut into thick slices

1 large red onion, cut into wedges

8oz/225g broccoli, cut into small florets

Vegetable Tempura

1 red pepper, deseeded and cut into strips

4oz/125g green beans, topped only (not tailed)

4oz/125g asparagus, trimmed

fresh basil leaves,

to garnish (optional)

sea salt

Method

Bring a saucepan of water to a boil. Add the eggs and boil for 10 minutes. Cool under cold running water, then remove the shells and finely chop the eggs.

Place the celeriac and chopped eggs in a large bowl. Mix together the olive oil, sesame oil and lemon juice and pour over the celeriac and eggs. Add the parsley, chives and seasoning, then mix thoroughly.

Ingredients

2 medium eggs

1lb 2oz/500g celeriac, grated

2 tbsp olive oil

1 tbsp sesame oil

juice of 1 lemon

3 tbsp chopped fresh parsley

3 tbsp snipped fresh chives

salt and black pepper

Celeriac and Herb Remoulade

Method

Preheat oven to 375°F/190°C.

Grease and line a Swiss roll (or lamington) tin and set aside. Wash the spinach several times to remove all grit, then steam or microwave (until soft). Squeeze thoroughly to remove all liquid. Chop very finely.

Place the spinach, nutmeg, chives, thyme leaves, butter, cream, egg yolks, and Parmesan cheese in a mixing bowl. Mix thoroughly and season (to taste) with salt and pepper. Beat the egg whites (until firm), then carefully fold into the spinach mixture. Spoon the spinach batter into the prepared tin, smoothing out the edges. Bake at 375°F/190°C for 12-15 minutes, until firm and "springy" to the touch.

Place a clean tea-towel on a flat surface and place the baked spinach-mixture face-down on the tea-towel and allow to cool slightly. The steam will help soften the batter, avoiding cracks when it is rolled later.

To make the filling: finely chop the olives, peppers, and tomatoes. Mix all the ingredients (except the artichokes) in a bowl and season (to taste) with salt and pepper. If necessary, soften the cream cheese to make it easier to blend. (Do not use a food processor because the vegetables will be too finely puréed.)

Remove the baked spinach mixture from the tin and paper and trim any tough edges. Spread with the cheese mixture and dot the finely sliced artichokes over the top. From the long edge, roll up the spinach and filling, using the tea-towel to help you. Once rolled, wrap the roulade in the tea-towel and chill for at least 6 hours.

To make the pesto: blend all the clives in a food processor with the basil leaves, breadcrumbs, and enough olive oil to correct the consistency. To serve, allow the roulade to come to room temperature and slice into 1in/2cm-thick portions. Serve with a spoonful of the Kalamata pesto on the side.

Ingredients

For Roulade

16oz/450g spinach or silverbeet	3 tbsp butter
¼ tsp nutmeg	3 tbsp heavy cream
1 bunch of chives, finely chopped	2 large eggs, separated
1 tsp fresh thyme leaves, chopped	3 tbsp Parmesan cheese, grated
	salt and pepper

Mediterranean Spinach and Herb Roulade with a Kalamata Olive Pesto

For Filling

2oz/50g Kalamata olives, pitted

2oz/50g sun-dried peppers

2oz/50g sun-dried tomatoes

6oz/180g cream cheese

2 tbsp sour cream

20 basil leaves, sliced

2 roasted artichokes, sliced

salt and pepper

For Pesto

10oz/300g Kalamata olives, pitted

1 bunch of basil

2 tbsp breadcrumbs

olive oil

starters

Method

Sauté the onion in 1 tablespoon of the oil until it begins to brown.

Beat the eggs in a bowl and add the broad beans, onion, pepper, salt, cumin, and basil. Mix well. Heat the remaining oil in an omelette pan, and pour in the egg mixture.

Turn the heat to low and cook for about 15 minutes. Either flip over as for frittata or place under a grill (broiler) to cook the top. Remove with an egg slicer.

Fava Bean Eggah

Ingredients

1 onion, finely sliced

¼ tsp pepper

2 tbsp olive oil

¼ tsp salt

6 eggs

1 tsp cumin

2 cups/12oz/350g fava beans, cooked

2 tbsp chopped basil or coriander (cilantro)

Method

Preheat oven to 350°F/180°C. Line a baking tray with nonstick baking paper. Set aside.

Filling: Place ricotta cheese, tomatoes, onion, basil, chives, lemon juice, and black pepper to taste in a bowl. Mix to combine.

Spoon filling into mushrooms. Place on prepared baking tray. Combine Parmesan cheese and breadcrumbs. Sprinkle over mushrooms. Bake for 10-15 minutes or until filling is set and top is golden.

Baked Ricotta Mushrooms

Ingredients

10 mushroom caps, stems removed

1 tbsp grated Parmesan cheese

1 tbsp dried breadcrumbs

Ricotta and Herb Filling

½ cup reduced-fat
fresh ricotta cheese

3 sun-dried tomatoes, soaked in warm water until soft, chopped

1 tbsp finely diced red onion

1 tbsp chopped fresh basil

1 tbsp snipped fresh chives

1 tsp lemon juice

freshly ground black pepper

Method

Preheat the oven to 425°F/220°C. Roll out the pastry and use it to line a 10in/ 25cm flan dish. Line with baking paper, fill with baking beans and cook for 15 minutes. Remove the paper and beans, then cook for another 5-10 minutes, until golden. Set aside. Reduce the temperature to 375°F/190°C.

Meanwhile, heat the oil in a wok or large, heavy-based frying pan. Add the scannions and stir-fry for 2-3 minutes, until they start to brown. Add the large open and oyster mushrooms and stir-fry for 3 minutes or until they begin to soften.

Pour in the wine and simmer for 6-8 minutes, until reduced slightly. Add all but a handful of the cranberries and boil for 1-2 minutes, until most of the liquid has evaporated and the cranberries begin to pop.

Blend the tofu, milk, and eggs to a smooth purée in a food processor or using a hand blender. Add the chives, lemon rind, juice, and seasoning and mix well. Spoon the mushroom mixture into the pastry case and pour over the tofu purée. Scatter with the remaining cranberries. Cook for 35 minutes or until golden and firm.

Mushroom and Cranberry Tart

Ingredients

12oz/350g shortcrust pastry, defrosted if frozen

2 tbsp sesame oil

bunch of scallions, chopped

9oz/250g large open mushrooms, finely sliced

4oz/125g pack oyster mushrooms, broken into large chunks

⅔ cup dry white wine

4oz/100g cranberries, defrosted if frozen

10oz/280g pack tofu

⅔ cup low fat milk or soya milk

2 medium eggs, lightly beaten

3 tbsp snipped fresh chives

grated rind and juice of ½ lemon

salt and black pepper

Method

Preheat an oven to 435°F/220°C.

Heat the butter and oil in a large frying pan and sauté the minced garlic and finely chopped onion. Meanwhile, finely chop the mushrooms in a food processor. Add these to the onion-mixture and cook gently for 5 minutes. Sprinkle the flour over the mushroom-mixture and stir to incorporate. Add the water or stock and stir until the mixture thickens and boils. Allow to cool thoroughly before adding the chopped chives and basil.

Lie a sheet of pastry on a flat surface. Spread one-sixth of the cooled mushroom-mixture over the pastry and sprinkle with one-sixth of the finely chopped nuts.

Fold opposite sides of the pastry in to meet in the middle, then fold again so that the pastry looks like a compact "log". Lie the log on its side and gently press down firmly. Slice the mushroom-filled log into 8 slices and lie each on a greased oven-tray. Repeat with remaining pastry and filling ingredients.

Freeze the uncooked pastry for five minutes, then bake at 435°F/220°C for 12-15 minutes (or until golden brown).

To make the herb-mayonnaise: mix the herbs and mayonnaise together and allow the flavors to blend for at least 30 minutes. Season with salt and pepper, and serve with the pastries.

Ingredients

1 tbsp butter

1 tbsp olive oil

2 cloves garlic (minced)

1 yellow onion (finely chopped)

7oz/200g wild mushrooms

(such as Swiss brown, porcini, shitake)

1 tbsp flour

2 tbsp water/stock

¼ cup chives (finely chopped)

¼ cup basil (finely chopped)

6 sheets puff pastry

¼ cup finely chopped pistachio nuts, toasted

2 tbsp coriander, finely chopped

2 tbsp chives, finely chopped

1 tbsp fresh parsley , finely chopped

½ cup good quality

purchased mayonnaise

salt and pepper (to taste)

Wild Mushroom Palmiers with Herb Mayonnaise

Note:

These pastries freeze well
(both cooked and uncooked),
so you can make these days
or weeks ahead and then defrost
and bake them (or refresh
in the oven) before serving.

starters

Method

Cook or microwave the pumpkin until just tender. Drain well and mash. For this recipe the pumpkin needs to be fairly dry. Stir the Parmesan cheese into the hot pumpkin, add salt and pepper and leave the mixture to cool. To make the ravioli, arrange four wonton wrappers on a board, brush edges lightly with the egg, then place one heaping teaspoon of pumpkin on each wrapper. Top each with a second wrapper, pressing the edges firmly together to secure. Cut the ravioli into circles using a 3 inch/7.5 cm biscuit (cookie) cutter.

Repeat this process until all the pumpkin is used. Bring a large pan of salted water to a boil and cook the ravioli for about 2-3 minutes, until al dente. Remove very carefully with a slotted spoon and drain (ravioli should be cooked in several batches). Place the oil in a clean pan, add the ravioli, dried tomatoes, and basil and swirl the pan very gently until the ravioli is coated with oil. Serve immediately.

Pumpkin Ravioli with Sun-Dried Tomatoes

Ingredients

18oz/500g butternut pumpkin

1 egg, beaten

¼ cup grated Parmesan cheese

3 tbsp virgin olive oil

salt and pepper

12-18 sun-dried tomatoes

8oz/250g packet wonton wrappers

2 tbsp chopped basil

Method

Soak the chickpeas in cold water for 12 hours, or overnight. Drain and rinse thoroughly, then place in a saucepan and cover with fresh water. Bring to a boil and cook for 10 minutes, removing any foam with a slotted spoon. Reduce the heat and simmer, covered, for 1 hour or until tender.

Drain the chickpeas, reserving 6 tablespoons of the cooking liquid, and set a few aside to garnish. Blend the remaining chickpeas to a fairly smooth purée with the reserved cooking liquid, the oil, and lemon juice in a food processor. Transfer to a bowl.

Place the tomatoes in a bowl and cover with boiling water. Leave for 30 seconds, then peel, deseed, and roughly chop. Add the tomatoes to the chickpea purée with the garlic, lemon rind, scallions (if using), parsley or mint, and seasoning.

Mix well and refrigerate for 30 minutes. Before serving, garnish with the reserved chickpeas and drizzle with olive oil, if desired.

Ingredients

9oz/250g dried chickpeas

6 tbsp olive oil, plus extra for drizzling (optional)

finely grated rind of ½ lemon and juice of 2 lemons

12oz/350g plum tomatoes

2 cloves garlic, crushed

2 scallions, finely chopped (optional)

3 tbsp finely chopped fresh parsley or mint

salt and black pepper

Creamy Chickpea and Tomato Dip

Method

Cut and seed the peppers and cut into large slices. Place these under a hot grill and cook (until the skins are blackened and blistered). Place the black peppers into a plastic bag and seal, allowing them to steam for thirty minutes. Remove the peppers from the bag and remove the skins. Set aside.

Slice the leek(s) lengthways and separate the leaves. Wash in cold water to remove all the grit, then plunge the largest cleaned leaves into a pot of boiling water.

Boil for 3 minutes, then remove the leek and rinse under cold water. Reserve the remaining leek for the garnish. Line a standard loaf tin with saran wrap, then drape the cooked leek leaves over the base and sides of the tin, allowing the long ends to hang over the sides.

Heat the butter and sauté the scallions (until softened). Mix the softened cream cheese, goat's cheese, herbs, scallion mixture and the salt & pepper in the large bowl of an electric mixture. Sprinkle the gelatin over the cold water and allow to soak for 1 minute. Place the gelatine mixture in the microwave and heat for 20 seconds on medium until the mixture is boiling (watching carefully to avoid its boiling over). Stir well with a fork. Add the dissolved gelatin and cream to the cheese mixture and mix to combine.

Pour one-third of the cheese mixture into the prepared loaf pan and cover with alternate red and yellow pepper slices. Cover with another third of the cheese

Ingredients

2 red peppers

2 yellow peppers

1 large (or 2 medium) leek(s)

4tbsp butter

1 bunch scallions

5 oz/150g cream cheese

10 oz/300g soft goat's cheese

½ cup Italian parsley, chopped

20 fresh basil leaves, torn

salt and pepper

2 tsp gelatin

1 tbsp cold water

10fl oz/300ml heavy cream

Vinaigrette

3 tbsp white wine vinegar

3 tbsp olive oil

½ tsp French mustard

½ tsp sugar

1 large tomato, seeded

1 medium cucumber, seeded

10 Kalamata olives, stoned

oil (for frying)

Terrine of Leek and Roasted Pepper with a Tomato Vinaigrette

mixture, repeating the pepper layer. Finish with remainder of cheese mixture, then drape the leek overhang back over the cheese filling to enclose. (Use any leftover leek to fill in the gaps if necessary.) Chill overnight.

Cut the remaining leek into very fine strips, then deep-fry them in hot oil (about 350°F/ 180°C) until golden. Drain the leeks on absorbent paper and store in an airtight container. Remove the terrine from the loaf tin and discard the saran wrap. Using an electric knife, slice thick, even portions of the terrine and serve accompanied by the vinaigrette.

To make the vinaigrette: whisk the vinegar, olive oil, mustard and sugar together until emulsified. Finely chop the tomato, cucumber, and olives, then mix together. Sprinkle the chopped vegetables around each slice of terrine on each individual plate and drizzle the vinaigrette over. Top with a tangle of deep-fried leeks.

starters

Method

Heat the oil in a wok or large, heavy-based frying pan. Add the shallots, garlic, and chili, if using, and stir-fry for 4-5 minutes, until they start to color. Add the sugar and the soy sauce and stir-fry for 3-4 minutes, until the shallots are evenly browned.

Add the vinegar and wine to the shallots and bring to a boil. Reduce the heat and simmer, uncovered, for 8 minutes or until the shallots have softened and the liquid has thickened and looks glossy. Add the asparagus, cover, and cook for 4-5 minutes, until tender, stirring occasionally.

Place the tomatoes in a bowl and cover with boiling water. Leave for 30 seconds, then peel, deseed, and chop. Add to the asparagus with the lemon juice, stir and heat for 1-2 minutes.

Meanwhile, preheat the grill to high. Toast the bread on both sides.

Serve the toast topped with the vegetable mixture and garnished with the parsley or coriander.

Ingredients

3 tbsp olive oil

10oz/300g bag shallots, thickly sliced

2 cloves garlic, thickly sliced

1 red chili, deseeded and

sliced (optional)

½ tbsp soft dark brown sugar

2 tbsp dark soy sauce

Caramelised Shallot and Asparagus Toasts

1 tbsp white wine vinegar or cider vinegar

white wine

4oz/100g pack asparagus tips

4 plum tomatoes

juice of ½ lemon

12 thick slices French bread

flat-leaf parsley or coriander

to garnish

Method

Place the eggplant, carrots, and red peppers in a bowl and season well.
(If you like you can use a vegetable peeler to make long ribbons with
the eggplant and carrots).

Toast the bread for 3 minutes each side or until golden brown. Meanwhile,
for the dressing, place the tomatoes in a bowl of boiling water for 30 seconds,
then peel, deseed, and finely chop.

Heat the sunflower oil in a large frying pan over a high heat, cook the vegetables
for 4 minutes, stirring all the time, until they have softened and are just tender.
Remove and set aside.

Heat the olive oil in the same pan and add the scallions and white
wine vinegar. Cook, stirring occasionally, for 1-2 minutes, until hot, then stir
in the tomatoes. Pile the vegetables on top of the toast, drizzle with
the hot dressing and serve.

Ingredients

2 eggplants, thinly sliced lengthways	1 tbsp sunflower oil
2 carrots, thinly sliced lengthways	2 tomatoes
2 red peppers, deseeded and thinly sliced	4 tbsp extra virgin olive oil
sea salt and freshly ground black pepper	2 scallions, sliced
4 thick slices stonebaked white bread	1 tbsp white wine vinegar

Vegetable Toast with Tomato Dressing

Method

Peel the potatoes, cut into cubes, and boil until tender. Drain and mash.
Crush garlic in a press or in a mortar with a pestle, add the salt, then
combine with mashed potato. A creamier consistency will be obtained
if the mixture is transferred to a food processor at this stage. While
mixing or beating the potatoes, add the olive oil gradually, then
the lemon juice and pepper.

Serve separately as a dip. Or, if you really want to impress,
heat and serve as a side dish to a main meal.

Skordalia (Potato Garlic Dip)

Ingredients

2lb/1kg potatoes

5 or more cloves garlic

1 tsp salt

⅔ cup olive oil

juice of ½ lemon

pepper

Method

Cook the chickpeas (garbanzo beans) in fresh water until tender, drain. Put all the ingredients except paprika and parsley into a food processor. Blend to a creamy paste. Serve on a plate dusted with paprika and garnished with parsley.

Hummus with Tahina

Ingredients

1 cup/5oz/150g chickpeas
(garbanzo beans), soaked

1 tsp salt

2 tbsp olive oil

4 tbsp tahina

1 tsp cumin seeds

juice of 2 lemons

1 tsp paprika

4 cloves garlic, crushed

parsley sprigs, to garnish

Method

Carrot and potato dip is a hearty starter to a barbecue meal.

It will keep your guests happy until the first barbecued treat is ready.

Boil the carrots, potatoes, and salt in water until the vegetables are soft. Drain and blend in a food processor with the garlic, cumin, chili, and lemon juice. Gradually add the oil and blend to a smooth, thick consistency.

Serve this spicy dip with fresh crusty bread or pita bread.

Ingredients

1½lb/750g carrots, chopped

1lb/500g potatoes, peeled and chopped

½ tsp salt

3 garlic cloves, chopped

4 tsp cumin seeds

1 chili, chopped

2 tbsp lemon juice

3 tbsp olive oil

Carrot & Potato Dip

Method

Line a colander or two large sieves with scalded muslin or cheesecloth and place over receptacle bowls to catch drainage.

Whisk the salt into the yogurt and pour into the colander or sieves. Leave to drain overnight; it will become a soft, creamy curd. Mould this into small rounds, place them on a perforated dish, and leave them in the refrigerator for 24 hours.

Note: The cheeses can be eaten straight away, sprinkled with the chopped herbs or paprika and served on slices of tomato.

If you want to keep them, leave them in the refrigerator for another 2-4 days, depending on how creamy you want them to be, then pack them into jars and cover with olive oil; store in a cool place.

Yogurt Cheese Balls in Olive Oil & Herbs

Ingredients

9 cups natural yogurt

2 tsp salt

finely chopped mint

finely chopped marjoram

finely chopped tarragon

paprika

olive oil

Method

Place the anchovy fillets and garlic in a bowl or mortar and grind to a pulp.
Add the oil, lemon juice, mayonnaise and cream, mix well and season to taste
with the pepper. Transfer to a decorative serving bowl and sprinkle with paprika.
Chill until ready to serve.

Provencal anchovy dip. The strong flavors of anchovies and garlic combine
in this dish to make an accompaniment to blander things, such as a raw
vegetable platter.

Homemade Mayonnaise

Place the eggs and the dry ingredients in a food processor or blender and blend
for 5 seconds. Then, with the machine still running, very gradually add the oil in
a thin, steady stream until the mixture is thick and creamy. Add the vinegar
and lemon juice and blend once more.

Makes 12fl oz/375ml.

Provençal Anchovy Dip

Ingredients

1oz/30g canned anchovy fillets, drained

1 clove garlic, roughly chopped

3 tbsp oil

1 tsp lemon juice

¼ cup homemade mayonnaise

¼ cup light cream

¼ tsp pepper

½ tsp paprika

Tip

The secret of making mayonnaise
is not to use cold ingredients; remove
eggs from the refrigerator a few hours
before use. The ingredients must be
beaten constantly and if the mixture
curdles, immediately add a few drops
of cold water.

Homemade Mayonnaise

Homemade Mayonnaise

2 eggs at room temperature

1 tsp dry mustard powder

1 tsp salt

1 tsp powdered sugar

¼ tsp cayenne

8fl oz/250ml oil

1 tbsp white vinegar

1 tbsp lemon juice

Method

Trim meat of all visible fat and cut into wafer-thin slices. Arrange beef slices, lettuce leaves and watercress attractively on four serving plates. Sprinkle with Parmesan cheese.

To make mayonnaise: place egg, lemon juice, garlic and mustard in a food processor or blender and process to combine. With machine running, slowly add oil and continue processing until mayonnaise thickens. Season to taste with black pepper.

Spoon a little mayonnaise over salad and serve immediately.

Mustard mayonnaise

1 egg

1 tbsp lemon juice

2 cloves garlic, crushed

2 tsp Dijon mustard

½cup olive oil

freshly ground black pepper

Ingredients

1lb/500g eye fillet beef, in one piece

1 lettuce, leaves separated and washed

1 bunch 8oz/250g watercress

3oz/90g Parmesan cheese, grated

Carpaccio with Mustard Mayonnaise

Tip

To achieve very thin slices

of beef, wrap the fillet in plastic

food wrap and place in the freezer

for 15 minutes or until firm,

then slice using a very

sharp knife.

starters

Method

To make filling: place pine nuts, prunes, apricots, ginger, sage, chutney, bacon, brandy and black pepper to taste in a food processor and process until finely chopped.

Open out steaks and pound to about ¼in/5mm thick. Spread filling over steaks and roll up tightly. Secure each roll with string.

Place stock, celery and onions in a large saucepan and bring to the boil. Add pork rolls, cover and simmer for 20 minutes or until pork is cooked. Transfer pork rolls to a plate, set aside to cool, then cover and refrigerate for 2-3 hours. To serve, cut each roll into slices.

Ingredients

fruit filling

2oz/60g pine nuts

3½ oz/100g pitted prunes

2oz/60g dried apricots

1 tbsp grated fresh ginger

1 tsp chopped fresh sage

3 tbsp fruit chutney

4 slices bacon, chopped

3 tbsp brandy

freshly ground black pepper

4 lean butterfly pork steaks

2 cups beef stock

4 stalks celery, chopped

2 onions, chopped

Fruity Pork Roulade

Method

Place the chicken wings in a shallow non-metallic dish and pour over the sauce. Squeeze the juice from 1 orange and pour into the empty sauce bottle. Give it a shake to release all the sauce, then pour the juice over the chicken. Turn the chicken to coat well, cover and place in the fridge to marinate for 10 minutes.

Preheat the grill to high. Place the chicken wings in a single layer on a large baking tray and pour over the marinade, reserving a little for basting. Grill the wings for 20 minutes, turning frequently and basting with the reserved marinade, until the flesh is cooked through and the skin is charred.

Meanwhile, peel the remaining oranges and divide into segments.

Divide the salad leaves between 4 plates, add the orange segments and spring onions and top with the hot chicken wings.

Spicy Chicken Wings with Orange

Ingredients

12 chicken wings

10oz/300g bottle Hoisin sauce

or barbecue sauce

3 oranges

5oz/130g bag green salad leaves

3 spring onions, sliced

Method

Brush the rocket or basil leaves with a little of the oil. Put a few in the middle of each ham slice, then place a breadstick in the center, leaving about 3in/7.5cm uncovered to use as a handle. Tightly wrap the ham around the breadstick, tucking it in neatly at the top. Brush the ham with the rest of the oil.

Breadsticks Wrapped in Parma Ham and Rocket

Ingredients

1oz/15g pack rocket or basil leaves

3 tbsp olive oil

6 thin slices Parma ham

6 breadsticks

69

Method

Soak the cellophane noodles in a bowlful of hot water to cover for 5-10 minutes (until tender), then drain immediately and rinse with cold water (to halt the cooking time). Cut noodles with scissors to a manageable length and toss with vinegar, fish sauce, crushed peanuts and shrimps.

Mix fresh herbs together and set aside. Finely shred the cabbage leaves and slice the spring onions into fine julienne. In a large bowl, mix together the herbs, cabbage leaves (both sorts), spring onions, noodle mixture and grated carrot (tossing thoroughly).

Working with 1 wrapper at a time, soak the rice wrapper in warm water for 30 seconds and lie on a flat surface. On each wrapper, place a small quantity of the mixed vegetable/noodle filling. Roll up tightly, folding the sides in, to enclose the filling. Continue rolling and folding until all ingredients are used.

To make the peanut sauce: heat the oil and sauté the garlic and minced chili until softened (about 2 minutes), then add all remaining ingredients and whisk (while heating). Bring to a boil and simmer until thickened slightly (about 3 minutes).

To serve, slice each roll on the diagonal, then rest one half over the other. Serve the sauce separately in a small pot for dipping.

Vietnamese Herb Salad Rolls with Home-Made Peanut Sauce

Ingredients

For Filling

2oz/50g packet cellophane noodles

3 tbsp rice vinegar

1 tbsp fish sauce

4 tbsp roasted peanuts (crushed)

12 large shrimp (cooked; finely chopped)

20 Thai basil leaves (finely sliced)

10 Asian mint leaves (finely sliced)

¼ fresh coriander (finely chopped)

4 leaves of Chinese cabbage (bok choy)

2 cabbage leaves (finely shredded)

5 spring onions

1 medium carrot (finely shredded)

12-16 rice paper wrappers (8in/20cm)

For Sauce

2 tbsp peanut oil

5 cloves garlic (minced)

½ small red chili (minced)

5 tbsp peanut butter

1½ tbsp tomato paste

3 tbsp hoisin sauce

1 tsp sugar

1 tsp fish sauce

¾ cup water

¼ cup peanuts (crushed)

Tip

As these wrappers do fry
successfully, you may like
to serve half of them fresh
and half of them fried.

starters

Method

Place pork, breadcrumbs, onion, garlic, oregano, cumin, chili powder and egg in a bowl and mix to combine.

Shape tablespoons of pork mixture into balls, place on a plate lined with plastic food wrap, cover and refrigerate for 30 minutes.

Preheat barbecue to a medium heat. Thread four balls onto a lightly oiled skewer. Repeat with remaining balls. Place skewers on lightly oiled barbecue grill and cook, turning frequently, for 8 minutes or until cooked through.

To make salsa: heat oil in a frying pan over a medium heat, add onion and cook, stirring, for 3 minutes or until onion is golden.

Add artichokes, tomatoes, tomato paste (purée) and oregano and cook, stirring, for 3-4 minutes longer or until heated through. Serve with skewers.

Ingredients

1lb/500g lean pork mince

1 cup/2oz/60g breadcrumbs, made from stale bread

1 onion, chopped

2 cloves garlic, crushed

1 tbsp chopped oregano

1 tsp ground cumin

½ tsp chili powder

1 egg, lightly beaten

Artichoke salsa

1 tbsp olive oil

1 onion, chopped

6oz/185g marinated artichoke hearts, chopped

4 tomatoes, seeded and chopped

2 tbsp tomato paste (purée)

1 tbsp chopped fresh oregano

Pork Skewers with Salsa

Method

Mix the chicken, veal, garlic and shallot in a blender, food grinder or processor (using the steel knife blade), until fine. Add the remaining ingredients except the bay leaves and grind everything until the mixture is smooth and the ham finely chopped. Place in a tureen with the bay leaves on top and bake in a preheated oven at 400°F/200°C) for 40 minutes or until the pâté pulls away from the sides and is brown on top.

Cover and refrigerate when cold. Serve with crusty French bread.

Ingredients

10oz/315g mixed raw chicken and veal

1 garlic clove, cut in half

1 shallot, cut in half

3 slices raw bacon, chopped

6 slices Parma ham, chopped

1 egg

1 tbsp brandy

a pinch each of salt, pepper and cinnamon

3 bay leaves

Pâté Maison

Pâté Maison

75

Method

Thai Marinade

A spicy marinade for satay sticks. Serve with the peanut recipe that follows.

Accompany with vegetable crudités and steamed rice.

Put all ingredients into a food processor and blend to a smooth paste. Marinate beef, pork, lamb or chicken for at least 2 hours. Thread onto skewers and grill. You can make a larger quantity and keep it refrigerated in a sealed jar.

Peanut Sauce for Satay

Serve this delicious sauce with satays or to accompany vegetable crudités. You can substitute peanut butter if you don't have time to roast and grind the peanuts yourself. There is a difference in flavor, though.

Place peanuts in a pan and roast in preheated oven at 375°F/190°C for 15 minutes. This will also loosen the skins. Remove from the oven and rub the skins off the peanuts. Grind the peanuts in a food processor.

Put onion in a pan with the oil and cook until it is translucent. Add garlic and chilies. Keep simmering and stir in the water, ground peanuts, cayenne, sugar and salt. When the sauce is smooth, stir in the soy sauce and lemon juice. Keep refrigerated, with a layer of oil on top to seal. It will keep for weeks.

Chicken Satay

Ingredients

Thai Marinade

1 tsp Thai curry paste

3 garlic cloves, chopped

1 tbsp soy sauce

1 tbsp chopped lemon grass

4fl oz/125ml coconut milk

Peanut Sauce for Satay

10oz/315g raw shelled peanuts

1 small onion, thinly sliced

1 tbsp oil; 3 chilies

3 garlic cloves, chopped

8fl oz/250ml water

¼ tsp cayenne; ½ tsp salt

½ tsp powdered sugar

1 tbsp soy sauce; 1 tbsp lemon juice

starters

Method

To clarify the butter: place it in a small saucepan and melt over a low heat for 3–4 minutes, taking care not to let it brown. Line a sieve with damp muslin, place over a bowl and pour the butter into the sieve, discarding the milky deposit left in the pan. Leave the strained liquid (clarified butter) to cool for 5-10 minutes. Meanwhile, blend the chicken or turkey and the ham until fairly smooth in a food processor. Add the pepper, nutmeg, allspice and cayenne to taste and blend until combined. Gradually pour in just under three-quarters of the clarified butter, blending all the time until mixed.

Spoon the mixture into small dishes or ramekins and top each with a bay leaf. Pour over the remaining butter to seal, then refrigerate for 2-3 hours, or overnight.

Potted Chicken and Ham

Ingredients

7oz/200g butter

7oz/200g cooked skinless chicken or turkey, cut into pieces

3½oz/100g cooked ham, cut into pieces

black pepper

¼ tsp ground nutmeg

pinch of ground allspice

pinch of cayenne pepper

4 fresh bay leaves

Method

Place chicken in a glass bowl, mix marinade ingredients together and pour over chicken. Cover and place in refrigerator to marinate for several hours or overnight.

Thread 2 tenderloins onto each skewer, using a weaving motion. Heat barbecue or electric grill to medium-high. Grease grill bars or plate lightly with oil.

Place skewers in a row, from left to right and cook for 2 minutes on each side, brushing with marinade as they cook and when turned. Remove to a large plate.

Serve immediately as finger food.

Ingredients

1lb/500g chicken tenderloins

Marinade

¼ cup/2fl oz/60ml teriyaki sauce

¼ cup/2fl oz/60ml honey

1 clove garlic, crushed

¼ tsp ginger, ground

small bamboo skewers, soaked

oil for greasing

Chicken Yakitori

starters

Method

Heat oil in a frying pan and sauté the almonds until pale gold in color. Quickly remove with a slotted spoon and drain on paper towel.

Add onion and fry until soft, stir in salt and spices and cook until aromatic.

Add chicken mince and stir-fry until almost cooked. Add chopped tomatoes, raisins, parsley, almonds and wine and simmer covered 15 minutes. Uncover and cook until juices are absorbed. Allow to cool.

Thaw the pastry according to packet instructions. Count out 14 sheets, repack and refreeze remainder.

Position pastry with long side parallel to bench edge in front of you. Cut into 3 even 6in/15.5cm wide strips. Stack and cover with clean tea towel. Take 2 strips at a time, spray each lightly with canola oil spray and fold in half, long side to long side. Spray surface with oil spray.

Place a teaspoon of filling on bottom end of each strip. Fold right-hand corner over to form a triangle then fold on the straight then on diagonal until end is reached. Repeat with remaining. Place on a tray sprayed with oil. Spray tops of triangles with oil and bake in a preheated moderate oven for 20-25 minutes. Serve hot as finger food.

Chicken and Almond Triangles

Ingredients

1 tbsp olive oil

½ cup/60g/2oz slivered almonds

1 medium onion, finely chopped

½ tsp salt

1 tsp ground cinnamon

1 tsp paprika

2 tsp ground cumin

1lb/500g chicken mince

2 small tomatoes, chopped

¼ cup/1½oz/45g raisins, chopped

2 tbsp finely chopped flat-leaf parsley

¼ cup/2fl oz/60ml dry white wine

1 packet filo pastry

canola oil spray

Tip

½lb/250g chicken stir-fry fried with 1 chopped onion, cooled

and mixed into ½lb/250g ricotta cheese

and 1 beaten egg.

Method

Heat oil in a small pan, add onion and garlic and fry until onion is soft.

Stir in curry paste and cook a little. Add lemon juice and stir to mix. Set aside.

Combine the mince, breadcrumbs, salt, pepper and coriander and add the onion/curry mixture. Mix well.

Place a thawed sheet of puff pastry on work surface and cut in half across the center.

Pile a ¼ of the mince mixture in a thick 1/2in/1 1/2cm wide strip along the center of the strip.

Brush the exposed pastry at the back with water, lift the front strip of pastry over the filling and roll to rest onto the back strip. Press lightly to seal. Cut the roll into 4 or 5 equal portions. Repeat with second half and then with second sheet. Glaze with milk and sprinkle with sesame seeds. Place onto a flat baking tray.

Cook in a preheated hot oven 370°F/190°C for 10 minutes, reduce heat to 350°F/180°C and continue cooking for 15 minutes until golden brown.

Serve hot as finger food.

Ingredients

2 tsp canola oil

1 medium onion, finely chopped

1 small clove garlic, crushed

2 tsp mild curry paste

1½ tbsp lemon juice

1lb/500g chicken mince

3 tbsp dried breadcrumbs

½ tsp salt

½ tsp pepper

2 tbsp chopped fresh coriander

2 sheets frozen puff pastry

1 tbsp milk for glazing

1 tbsp sesame seeds

Curried Chicken Rolls

starters

Tip

May be made in advance and reheated

in a moderate oven.

Method

To make the marinade: whisk together the rice vinegar, lime juice, chopped coriander and ginger. Cut the salmon fillet into finger-sized pieces, each about 3in x 1in/8cm x 2cm. (You should have 12 pieces.) Place these into the marinade and allow to marinate (for 30 minutes).

To make the dipping-sauce: (while the salmon marinates) In a small bowl, whisk together the lime juice, rice vinegar, soy sauce, fish sauce, sugar, ginger, coriander and parsley. Alternatively, for a smoother sauce, process all these ingredients briefly (until the herbs are finely chopped). Set aside.

Meanwhile, cut the spring onions into 3in/8cm lengths, then finely slice the spring onions into thin strips. Peel the carrot, cut into 3in/8cm lengths and then julienne the carrot into thin strips.

Remove the salmon from marinade and pat dry.

Fill a large bowl with warm water and soak the rice-paper wrappers (one at a time) until softened. When one wrapper is soft, place it on a clean tea-towel and place a piece of salmon on top. Add some strips of spring onion, carrot and some coriander leaves, then roll up the filling tightly, folding the sides in as you roll. Place the rolled-up spring roll on the seam and repeat the soaking, rolling and folding (until all the ingredients have been used).

To cook the salmon rolls, heat some peanut oil to a depth of 1in/2cm. Fry the rolls, seam-side down (until golden underneath), then turn and cook the other side. Drain on absorbent paper, then serve immediately with the dipping-sauce.

Ingredients

For Salmon

¼ cup seasoned rice vinegar

¼ cup fresh lime juice

2 tbsp fresh coriander (chopped)

1 tsp ginger-root (fresh; peeled; grated)

1lb/500g piece of salmon (skin removed)

4 spring onions

1 carrot

12 rounds of rice-paper wrappers

½ bunch fresh coriander

peanut oil (for frying)

Fresh Salmon Spring Rolls with Herb Dipping-Sauce

For Sauce

3 tbsp lime juice (fresh)

2 tbsp rice vinegar

1 tbsp soy sauce

1 tbsp fish sauce

2 tsp sugar

2 tsp ginger (fresh; grated)

½ cup coriander (fresh)

2 tbsp parsley (fresh)

Method

Place ricotta cheese, dill and yogurt in bowl. Mix to combine.
Set aside.

Spread lavash bread with mustard. Top with salmon. Spread
with ricotta mixture – leave 4in/10 cm at one short end uncovered.
Sprinkle with lemon juice and black pepper to taste.

Starting at the covered short end, roll up firmly. Wrap in plastic
food wrap. Refrigerate for several hours or until ready to serve.

To serve, cut rolls into 1in/2 cm thick slices. Arrange attractively
on a serving platter.

Gravlax Spirals

Ingredients

½ cup/125g reduced-fat ricotta cheese

3 tbsp chopped fresh dill

½ cup/100g low fat natural yogurt

2 slices lavash bread

¼ cup/60ml honey mustard

3oz/100g gravlax, smoked salmon
or smoked ocean trout

lemon juice

freshly ground black pepper

Method

Smoked Fish Flan

Make this with any type of smoked fish, such as haddock, cod or trout.

It is absolutely delicious.

Line a flan tin (pie pan) or dish with the pastry and chill for 30 minutes.

Place the flaked fish in the pastry case (pie shell). Put the rest of the ingredients into a bowl and whisk them together. Pour this mixture over the fish.

Bake the flan in a preheated oven at 375°F/190°C for 30-40 minutes.

Shortcrust Pastry (Basic Pie Dough)

Sift the flour and salt into a bowl. Cut the butter into small pieces and add to the bowl. Rub the butter into the flour with your fingertips until the butter is completely absorbed and the texture resembles breadcrumbs. Mix the egg yolk with the water and lemon juice. Make a well in the flour, add the liquid and mix together with your fingertips to form a ball. Add more moisture if it gets too dry. Put the dough on a floured surface and knead it lightly with the palms of your hands until it is smooth.

Wrap in clingfilm (plastic wrap) and chill for 30 minutes or up to 3 days. (It can also be frozen.) Put the dough on a floured surface and roll it out with a floured rolling pin. Line the flan tin (pie pan) or dish and chill before filling and baking.

Smoked Fish Flan

Ingredients

1 quantity shortcrust pastry

¼ cup/1oz/30g Parmesan cheese

8oz/225g cooked and flaked smoked fish

salt and pepper

¾ cup/6fl oz/175ml heavy (thick) cream

1 tsp fennel seeds

3 egg yolks, beaten

Shortcrust Pastry (Basic Pie Dough)

7oz/200g/1¾ cup flour, sifted

2 tsp iced water

¼ tsp salt

lemon juice

4oz/125g/½ cup butter

egg wash (beaten egg yolk)

1 egg yolk

Tip:

You can use any smoked fish

type for this dish, for example

mackerel or front.

starters

Method

Blend shrimp, garlic, egg, cornstarch, oil and soy sauce to a paste in a food processor. Alternatively, grind shrimps with a pestle and mortar, then mix with the other ingredients.

Spread one side of each slice of bread evenly with prawn paste, sprinkle with sesame seeds, remove crusts and cut into 4 triangles. To make dipping sauce, mix together ginger, chili sauce and lime juice, then set aside.

Heat 1in/2.5cm of oil in a large frying pan over a medium to high heat. Add half the shrimp triangles, shrimp-side down, and fry for 4–5 minutes on each side, until deep golden. Drain on towel paper and keep warm while you cook the remaining shrimp triangles. Serve with dipping sauce.

Sesame Shrimp Triangles with Chili Sauce

Ingredients

4oz/115g cooked peeled shrimp, defrosted if frozen

1 clove garlic, chopped

2 tbsp beaten egg

1 tsp cornstarch

½ tsp sesame oil

a few drops of light soy sauce

3 slices of white bread

2 tbsp sesame seeds

groundnut oil for deep-frying

Dipping Sauce

½in/1cm piece fresh root ginger, finely chopped

2 tbsp hot chili sauce

juice of ½ lime

Method

Slash the sardines diagonally 3 or 4 times on each side, using a sharp knife. Mix together the oil, orange rind and seasoning, add the sardines and turn to coat. Cover and place in the fridge for 30 minutes.

To make the relish: Slice the top and bottom off each orange with a sharp knife, then cut off the skin and pith, following the curve of the fruit. Cut between the membranes to release the segments, then chop into ½ in/1cm (Áin) pieces. Mix with the spring onions, chilies, dill, capers and oil.

Preheat the grill to high. Put the sardines onto the grill rack, reserving the marinade. Grill for 3 minutes on each side, brushing occasionally with the marinade, or until the flesh has turned opaque and the skin has browned. Garnish with dill and serve with the relish.

Ingredients

12 fresh sardines, scaled and gutted

3 tbsp olive oil

finely grated rind of 1 orange

salt and black pepper

Grilled Sardines with Orange and Dill Relish

For the relish

4 large oranges

bunch of spring onions,
finely sliced

1-2 red chilies, deseeded and finely chopped

3 tbsp chopped dill, plus
extra to garnish

2 tbsp capers, rinsed
and drained

1-2 tbsp extra virgin olive oil

starters

Index